POEMS FROM AN ORDINARY MAN

SOME LIGHT HEARTED SOME MORE DARK
SOME CAME STRAIGHT FROM MY HEART

STUART ALEXANDER HAYWARD

Copyright © 2023 Stuart Alexander Hayward

©2023 Stuart Alexander Hayward all rights reserved.

The characters and events portrayed in this book are fictitious. Any similarity to real persons, living or dead, is coincidental and not intended by the author.

No part of this book may be reproduced, or stored in a retrieval system, or transmitted in any form or by any means, electronic, mechanical, photocopying, recording, or otherwise, without express written permission of the publisher.

Cover design by: Stuart Alexander Hayward

This book is dedicated to all the family and friends that supported my writings over the years, especially my number one fans, my wife and my MUM and DAD.
It has made it much more easier to continue writing my poems knowing that there are people out there that do enjoy reading them.
To the small group of freinds who have supported me from the early poems and songs I am truly grateful. You know who you are.
To you all, I thank you very, very much.

Stu

CONTENTS

Title Page
Copyright
Dedication
Introduction
2020	1
Real	4
Allotment	5
Football	6
Mablethorpe	8
Weeds	9
Kids	10
Allotment 2	11
Man with the crooked smile	12
Big un	13
Splend	15
Poker	16
You	17
Omicron	19
Teenage Summer	21
Allotment 3	24
Time	25

My Book	27
Contemplation	29
Dad	31
Family	33
Sorrow	35
Mum	37
Happy	39
Goodnight	41
Greenhouse	43
Tired	45
Words	47
Till	49
The Nod	50
Happy Birthday	52
Allotment 4	54
Good Night	55
Golf	57
Autumn	59
My Mam	60
I Didn't Know	62
Never Give Up	64
December	65
Do it	67
Manchester	68
Far away	69
Jan 1	71
Don't	73
Remember	74

Calm	75
Life	77
Snow	79
Hit it	81
Worry	83
Blossom	85
Dark	87
Bored	89
Age	91
Lightening	93
Moon	95
How Long	96
Wealth	98
Sea	100
Wet	102
Gobby	103
Another Day	104
Puppy	105
More Words	106
Snooze	107
Today	108
Misty	110
Beauty	112
Sorry	113
Mo	115
Fear	116
Prostate	118
Cancer	120

Aftermath	121
Acknowledgement	123
About The Author	125
Books By This Author	127

INTRODUCTION

The following book contains poems, verses and you may even call one or two short stories. As the title says, I am an ordinary man and these poems are varied in what they are about as well as how I have written them.
I have not got a degree in English Literature so please read them for what they are.

What they are, are words put down from a man telling stories or sharing his thoughts as he hears them in his head or feels them in his heart. Some are written from memories I hold dear and some from pain I have not forgotten. Most come from being in the now at that moment in time.

The poems have been written across several years of my life in which I have been through highs and lows, good times and bad times.
I hope you read them and maybe one or two may just put a smile on your face or give you a bit of hope in that your not on your own in what you sometimes feel. Some may even bring a tear to your cheek.

Some are very personal and about friends and family I love very much. These poems I have put in the book because I love the people so much and it is a statement of that love as to why they are in the book.

The last few poems in the book were written during the period of time I was going through finding out I have prostate cancer.

My hopes are you will read my book of poems and you will find favourites that you will read over and over, but you may also read ones that may upset you and if that happens then I am sorry for that as that is not my intention. As the tital page says these poems range from happy and light hearted to some more dark and meaningful.

You will find your way through this book reading as you go as I did writing it as I went, and it is my hope that you will enjoy what you read.

Stu

2020

It started slow, not much snow
In it came, as we thought, just the same
But we were wrong
On its way, it's not going to be fun
The pain it will bring, it's going to sting

The virus was coming

We were all so blind, singing songs
Eating food, and drinking booze
Party time, it was just a rouse

The virus was coming

January went, February the same
March started to kill, the virus to blame
Everyone panicked, the bog rolls just vanished
Beans left the shelves, along with hand wipes and gels

The virus is here

Government warnings, they just weren't clear
Not like the visors, now wrapped around our ears
Some people listened, but mostly they didn't
The hospitals got busy
We clapped for the doctors, and the nurses now in a tizzy

The virus is here, it was now getting busy

Lockdown came, the streets were empty
Hospitals struggled to manage the plenty
R number high, it didn't look good
Then It started to drop, started to look better

STUART ALEXANDER HAYWARD

The virus is here, it was trying to get ya

Holiday booked, ready to go
The government not happy they said no
Ryan air, he flew his planes empty
No money back, though he charged us plenty

The virus is here, still infecting the many

Now we have tears, not just on our cheeks
Tear four is the worst, we're just still in three
No meeting, no touching, just stay in your bubble
It really is hard, I just want a cuddle

The virus is here, nasty and changing

Christmas has been, not many people seen
But if you have had it, and your still in one peace
Just share a thought, for people buried deep
Plenty didn't make it, no tinsel no crackers
Let's raise a glass, and remember, because it matters

The virus is here, but let battle commence

New Year's Eve, sat thinking plenty
Beers on the go, and snacks on the table
Let's rage war on the virus, the vaccines are able
Stick one in my arm, and let normal commence

The virus is here, but let's hope not for long

But what now is normal
I just can't remember
Pubs have all closed
Got rid of the last member
It's still raging hard, but the vaccine is here
Let's give it chance, so we can celebrate properly
So happy new year, to you and to yours

Let's raise a glass, and sing a cheer
Hold on tight, if need be then shed a tear
Let's just hope, we're all here this time next year

Stu

REAL

Sometimes I feel, like none of this is real
Sometimes I feel, like letting out a scream, shout or squeal
Sometimes I feel, like everyday is an ordeal
Sometimes I feel, like the pain is all I feel

But this is life
But this is real
But so what, if you scream, shout or squeal
But it's the other side of the ordeal
But sometimes, pain is what you have to feel

She knows it's real
She needs to scream, shout or squeal
She can't get through the ordeal
She feels the pain
She wants to be without having to feel

Enjoy your life
Enjoy now is real
Enjoy the scream, shout or squeal
Enjoy the ordeal
Enjoy the pain
Enjoy the feel
Enjoy your life its yours you are the real deal

Stu

ALLOTMENT

We got an allotment, from the father in law
Grown really high, couldn't get through the door
The nettles so high, we can't see the floor
Think we need a strimmer, to cut them down, one an all

The nettles so green, they grow so tall
The best thing to do, is pull them from the floor
Wear thick gloves, the stingers are the worst
If they brush against your skin, I guarantee it hurts

Then there's the brambles, thick long and hard
These are the big beasts, thorns so very sharp
Even the thick gloves can't protect you from these barbs
Grab them down the wrong way, and find out just how sharp

Days and days we've pulled at these weeds
It's only now with broken backs, we get to sit and read
Trying to chill, and enjoy the new plot
But what about the planting, nothing grows if nobody sews

Stu

FOOTBALL

(euros21)

The ones that just don't get it
Say it's only a game
Yes that is true it is only a game to you
But to some to most it's just so much more

It's ecstasy it's agony it's envy it's jealousy
It's a smile it's a grimace it's a frown it's the limit
Makes you want to laugh makes you want to cry
Makes you groan makes you want to die

We conquered the world never done it since
We try we try we try
Never get there but why oh why
They give it there all without a sigh

We score first they don't like that
They come back we can't hack that
They score back it's even now
Lets try hard extra time is here

Time has gone we're tired out
Subs are on they've all been made
Who will stand up and be so strong
It's really not easy to do what they've done

Some will score some will miss
Some will be saved and some will be weak as piss
They all tried their best so give them respect
Could you do better in your stained vest

It was a good try furthest we've been
Furthest most people have ever seen
We just didn't get there but we were so close
Chins up my friends the journey never ends
Wait while next year the pain will be even more real
Dont be so lame
It's only a game

Stu

MABLETHORPE

Got here Monday long drive we had
Arrived at the caravan with little food but lots of drink and crap

Unpacked in a jiffy and off to the beach
Nice in the sun I don't want to preach
Dogs panting sons ranting where's all the bars for boozing

Had a drink or two then back to the shack
Let's get ready for eating there's a snap hole over there at the back
Got there it's shut what shall we do off to
another there's at least two

Oh no again this is shut too
What about takeaway there has to be a few
Beep beep it's busy but for the last hour nearly two
Let's go to the site bar we can eat and drink a few

But oh dear me nobody told us you see it's Mablethorpe
Monday but what does that mean it's if your very hungry
the food shops are shut so go eat your crisps and maybe
some nuts it's Mablethorpe Monday everything's shut

Stu

WEEDS

Hoe the weeds before they grow
For if you don't they will let you know
Just how fast they can grow
Turn your back and let them go
In no time at all they will be all over the show
So help yourself out and use the hoe
Just don't let those buggers grow.

Stu

KIDS

As a kid the world is blue
There's the sky no clouds to spoil the view
You want to play so that's what you do
You meet your mates there the same as you

Out you go to play you won't be alone they will be here soon
Your friends are here they are playing with you
Your playing with them it's what you all do
Until your no longer young now they don't live near you

At school there were lots of kids
You knew a few not them all and some knew you
So you would play with kids you knew
You had best friends just a few

Time goes by your not a kid anymore
The friends you had are fewer than they were before
But if your lucky you kept in touch with a few
Most of us have that one that never flew

So keep in touch send that text
Don't hold back don't waist time
It's not hard to do make the move let them know it's you
It will make them happy you'll see it's true

Stu

ALLOTMENT 2

We plant the seeds some say we sew
Into the ground hoping they will grow
Days will pass a week or two may go
But then you turn up and look what's grown

The soil you've watered every day
Has now been pushed to the side out of the way
But why for what you say
Because those seeds have grown
They are here and here to stay

The green of plants in the soil to see
So bright and lush a pleasure to be
Now their there we can see our work
Get that can full of water and watch it spurt

Keep them moist and watch them grow
Every day you can see them go
Higher and bigger and look now there's fruit
Harvest those plants to eat even the root

Stu

MAN WITH THE CROOKED SMILE

He's the man with a crooked smile
He's gonna laugh and joke just for a while
When he sees you get ready to smile
Cos he's the man with the crooked smile

He's gonna play you a song in a minute
While he strums his guitar it's electric
Sings his songs not very good there all covers
He's the man with the crooked smile

Come to his garden there are beers flowing
Karaoke everyone is singing
Sniffing snuff all their eyes are streaming
Cos he's the man with a crooked smile

Later on all the beers still flowing
Pissed as farts in his garden suns going
The Jacuzzi is all hot bubbles blowing
He's the man with the crooked man with the
crooked man with the crooked smile.

Stu

BIG UN

Big Un
Can be quiet can be loud
Always very proud
All ways right never wrong likes to work to the tune of a song
Doesn't talk shite always very bright
Big Un

Slings the hammer and rattles the spanners
Hands been smashed but keeps on swinging
Won't be beat likes a treat sometimes not so sweet
Says it as it is don't like it don't listen
Big Un

Went to the gym got big un strong
Shoulders massive not many can compete
Come and try and he'll put you in a seat
Not so young packed in the gym
Rides a bike goes for miles
Goes even further with an electric convertor
Big Un

Mellowed out with age, that can't be escaped
Likes to sing a song with a Stetson on
Doesn't ride a horse prefers two wheels down the Forrest course
He has got the rhythm there is no doubt and
always try's to give it some clout
Big Un

Used to see him four times a week
Now it's very rare we speak
He's always there at the end of the phone

Will answer my message every time without a groan
Big un

Stu

SPLEND

Back in the day people would say
How's tha get that quiff so stiff
Smile on his face flick of the head
Not easy young en would quickly be said

Lovely quiff so slick and stiff
Smile always on banter always strong
Loves the crack never slack
Likes his work always there
Going out never on time but always starts with a funny rhyme

Coming out ready for seven be there for eight always late
Park your car at his garden gate
Hoot the horn here he comes
Oh no he's gone back in will he come before were gone

Now he's here funny quips galore
Smiles and giggles even more
He keeps them coming no matter the score

Likes to sing a song
Likes a game of poker
Likes to work late
Likes to drink a beer
Used to love a quiff
Used to love a spliff
Splend.

Stu

POKER

I may not be pretty, I can not sing,
But baby I'm here to play poker, and here to win
So put your money in, and deal those cards
because baby I'm here, just you watch the sparks
I got a pocket pair, the flop makes trips
I'll wait for the river to hit two less than six
I'm going all in, your full house ain't enough
I've got all four, and for you, that's just tough

Stu

YOU

Don't try to be the person that your not
Your not him and he's not your lot
Be happy with the one the one that you are
Don't waste time trying to change any part
Cos change ain't going to put you in a happy place

It's you, you, you, you are the one
Don't run away and don't try to change
Just be happy with what you've got
Because if your not you will lose the plot

Celebrate just who you are
Don't listen to the people who say your no good
They don't know the journey that you've took
You've driven the car that they could not steer
You just keep on going and never show your fear

So stand up strong show just who you are
Let them see your strength let them see it from afar
Your better when your you so stand up strong
The taller that you stand the less they will demand

Don't let them bend you because that's not right
The shoes you stand in have been through the fight
They never wore them they just wouldn't fit
There your shoes the perfect fit

Now you know you don't have to change
Nobody's perfect though some think they are
Your certainly not but there your scars
Don't hurt them they won't hurt you

But If they give you some shit just throw it back

Let's live this life through and through
Why make it hard stick to the truth
Just walk away if they don't like you
Friends are precious this is true
Enjoy the ones that are there for you

Stu

OMICRON

It came and went or so we thought
Lock downs in you can't watch sport
It went rife and spoilt our life
What could we do, defcon one then defcon two

Out you go numbers are down
Take of your mask without a frown
All feels good but it's all too soon
Numbers back up like a balloon

The old virus has gone but here comes Omicron
This ones bad the numbers say it all
One hundred thousand a day or so they say
Falling like flies from the virus we despise

Bit of a cough and a banging head
Pain in the chest I better take the test
Tickle the tonsils and up the nose
Gipping like mad curling my toes

Ten minutes later the lines make their show
We only want one then we can go
The time it's took it should read like a book
The results are clear looks like I'm stuck in here

Waitress fed my wife brings me food in bed
It ain't no fun eating tablets like bullets from a gun
They null the pain but the bedrooms becoming a drain
Im trying really hard not to go insane

Two days to go to Christmas morning
I'm going to see it from my bed still yawning
I'm not that bad I'm not hospital bound
Be thankful for small mercies that's what I've found

STUART ALEXANDER HAYWARD

So chins up on this holiday season
Lets have a beer we don't need a reason
Have a few more line them up on the floor
When you feel dizzy eat some food open a pressie
Merry Christmas one and all

Stu

TEENAGE SUMMER

Do you remember the first time that you fell in love
It was summer and I felt like I could fly like a dove
Never felt like this before too young to even know the score
I'd only just stepped out of my parents front door

Too young to know what is was
Too young to know what it meant
You just new it felt strong just like cement

The feelings were strong they felt so raw
The summer came it felt so warm
You and friends on holiday
the first Away from your parents claws

Young and free in a caravan down by the sea
You and two mates made three
We didn't need any more
The caravan wouldn't take four

Drinking beers getting drunk
Not yet 18 the caravan stunk
Drinking beers singing songs
Meeting people making friends

Having fun everyday
Still so young oh how we would play
Our hearts were big
They had never been broken
Girls back then never out spoken

You met the one
Others hadn't come close
Big blue eyes and a sexy little nose
Smile brighter than any rose
She didn't even need to pose

Would it work you didn't care
She lived so far but god that stare
No internet no face book
Writing letters was all it took

It felt so good what will the letter say
It was all about what she'd done that day
So young so free
Your first love was what she'd be
You were both just so full of glee

The letters came you wrote everyday
You even partied on a weekend stay
But the distance didn't help to play

Then it came the one not so nice
The nasty letter you read more than twice
Your heart so big now broke into pieces
So that's what love was you'd heard all the stories
But now you had the tears on your cheek
They came from your eyes
It was them that now leaked

Dust yourself down it would never have worked
Too many miles you new from the start
Now it was winter you had a new heart

All mended full and ready to go
But never forget that first time that it broke

Stu

ALLOTMENT 3

The plots coming on weeds nearly gone
We're now getting green that's wanted to be seen
We've dug another square now the weeds are bare
We didn't use the spade the machine stops the back ache

Another patch ready for seeds now we've got rid of the weeds
The soil so soft it's ready for planting
The dog thinks it's hers she just sits there watching us planting
She's now a lottie doggie loves it to death

She's made so many friends
She thinks she's the queen
She's walks tail wagging
She looks like she's bragging
She knows where to go
She's on an adventure don't you know

She can't do any planting with the four legs she's got
But after her running she's panting a lot
Up and down she goes inspecting it all
But then she sits down on soil that's warm
That's her done ready for home
But she will be back to see what has grown

Stu

TIME

How many bricks have we got
We've got six and that's our lot
Is six enough to build that ramp
We have no more how far will we land

Mirror signal manoeuvre every time
Practise makes perfect you'll be fine
Driving a car is much faster than my bike
Keep taking lessons on your test you will fly

School was ok we learnt dribs n drabs
Never took it serious was always after a laugh
But collage is here and this is real tuff
It's time to learn a job that will pay for all my stuff

Time we going to meet eight under the clock
It's Friday night we're going out for a drink
listen to the music rock
This week it's wakey such a buzz going on in the eighties
Next week it's donny suited and booted always loud never muted

With this ring I thee wed your so stunning in your dress
Married life isn't all bliss but when it's you
it can't get better than this
The jell will be cold on your tummy
Just watch the screen with eyes soon to be runny

Giving birth we went to hell and back
Daughter was the first with our son soon to follow
Tunisia Tenerife Disney land the lot
So many holidays all so hot

Blink of an eye daughters at uni clever tall

and thin an absolute beauty
Sons now at college growing big and strong
turning into a lovely young man
How did we get here where has it gone
What a great life don't worry about things that went wrong

Time is ticking it can't be stopped enjoy
every second don't be robbed
Yesterday a child no worries at all
Today a lot older with weight on your shoulder
Look what you've done a wife a daughter a son
You can't change the past or see into the future
Enjoy this rhyme
you
can't
stop
TIME

Stu

MY BOOK

Life is lite or so they say
It's all so easy when it feels like play
But the cover does not tell the story of the book
One quick glance or even a look
Does not tell the story of my book

Do not think how I look defines the story of my book
Fore what you see can be mistook
I look so strong I look so tough
But that's not the story in my book
You need to look closer to really look
Then you may see just a glimpse of what's in my book

Normal as we knew it was overtook
What it was now gone this changed everybody's book
The essence of man nearly destroyed in this world
The pandemic came the darkness fell
Millions of people going through hell

What doesn't kill you makes you stronger
But when your stuck inside just wanting to take the next big stride
Thoughts in your mind you just can't hide
Words in your book you don't want to write
But the pen won't stop it's a very hard fight

You are you and no one else
This is good enough tell yourself
Times will be hard times will be good
You'll get through them all like you know you should
Don't sit and dwell because the darkness will take you back to hell
Stand up take a bow look in the mirror and scream out wow

Nobody is better nobody is worse
There is no such thing as a curse

Life can be hard life can be tuff
But you know your made of better stuff
It's your book to write so hold on tight
Make your story one to tell send the darkness into hell
So just make sure on the next page is kindness and joy
There's no room for all that rage
Send it with the darkness from this page
Then the book that you write comes from words that you like
With all the stories you deserve enjoy your life and all the perks
It's your book no one else's please make sure you fill in all the pages

Stu

CONTEMPLATION

Time on your hands what shall I do
Time doesn't stop not even for you
You don't have to be busy
You don't always have to do
The list of jobs will wait for you

When your sat just you on your own
When contemplation comes
You know your in the zone
Write down what comes
Could be bad or could be good
Once written down it's all yours
No need to sign in blood

What's in your mind is it empty or full
Are you thinking about life
Or about what you want to do
Enjoy this time it's there just for you
Enjoy contemplation make it your friend
Then you will find it's easy to unwind

Let your thoughts wonder or don't think at all
Enjoy contemplation with thoughts large or small
Get lost in those thoughts and enjoy them one and all
From childhood to nightclubs you've made them all
Just enjoy the moment you deserve it its yours

So what did you learn sat on your own
In your own head lost in the zone
No need to hurry lost all the worry
Contemplation in buckets
Leave the worry for the muppets

Contemplation over what now is different
Look over your shoulder then you will see
It's all just the same for you and for me
So when those minutes are spare
You know there so rare don't let them pass
Enjoy them all whether large or small
Nothing will change I guarantee this is true
Enjoy contemplation it's there just for you

Stu

DAD

Your my dad I even look like you
You don't know the love we all have for you
You know you've done well
When your sons adore you

I look in the mirror and what do I see
I see you looking right back at me
Oh my god I look like my dad
Some say his double now that's not bad

From Scotland he came down on a train
His wife he met small blonde and hard to get
But try he wood until she understood
No wasn't the answer that he took

Married they were how long would they last
Nearly sixty years not always been a blast
But laugh and cry they've seen it all
Problems large and problems small
But they have lived through them all
Still here to tell the stories one and all

We're all here for this great man
A husband a father a grandad even great
All this family came from you
We love adore and think your the best
Truly the best father I do have to say
I hope I'm just like you in the best possible way

So my fine fellows on this fine day
Happy 80th birthday we'd all like to say
So let's raise a glass and take in a drink
Cheers enjoy this it's all for you

From your loving family and your
Eldest son

Stu

FAMILY

Family and friends they are the key
That's where we're going
Who will we see
Up there in Scotland
Thats where well be

Over the wall jump it's not that high
There's not much left Hadrian would cry
But when my mum says
Get back over the wall
Back where you came from
My dad he just laughs
My mum shes so small

Glasgow we're bound
Family their sound
Big Rabs the man
Does all that he can
Got us the tickets
For the match we will see
We are so lucky
For our family so sweat

He won't take a shilling
He won't take a pound
Let's buy him a drink

He stands there so proud
A big man a proud man
A heart made of gold
This is big Rab he's
Everything we were told

Sharon and Andrea
Their mum and their dad
We grew up together though miles apart
This doesn't matter when their
Always in your heart
Not often we see them
But boy when we do
Let's have a party
For us and for you

A celebration to have
A beer or two
This could get messy
More beers more than a few
Let's just keep drinking
The company's the best
We'll worry about the hangover
Tomorrow while we rest

So raise up your glasses
Let's enjoy this time
One man that's missing
Always in our minds
Campbells his name
A great man a loved man
A father a grandad a friend
He will always be missed
So cheers to family
Lets all get pissed

Stu

SORROW

Sorrow comes from many sources
Some so small people wouldn't think
That something like that could cause such a stink

It creeps in slow but steels the show
Sometimes so fast how long will it last
Nobody knows how sorrow grows
But it grows then through your face
That's where it shows

Then grow it does consumes your life
Like it never should
What do you do when sorrow takes over you

Live your life like you should
Sorrow doesn't care
Why do you think it even should
It will hurt and disable you
It just seems like there's nothing you can do

Take it on you have to be strong
It won't be easy it will make you queasy
But when you know why it's there
Then you can fight because then it's fair

Once you know the reason why
Now the tears can start to dry
They won't stop running straight away
But at least now they don't show every day

Time is a healer so they say
But sorrow only goes
When you take a stand
And you tell it it's time to go away

There's never a time you think that's right
Always a struggle always a fight
But time has passed
You've fought with sorrow day and night
So nows your time to win this fight

Standup strong you've earned the right
It won't go away not overnight
But this is the time to say goodnight
Time to move on and turn sadness into light

Stu

MUM

In your tummy so warm and soft
Kicking and moving keeping you up
My own little home you supplied without fuss
No rent to pay not much room to play

Carry me you did for 9 long months
Then out I came your life never the same
Such a small bundle helpless and loud
Pooing and peeing but made you so proud

Every day your care was never questioned
Changing the nappies cleaning my bum
Making me smile from tickling my tum
These are just a few things that you have done

As I grew older the more that you did
Cleaning my clothes and meals galore
Every day never relenting a little power house
Sometimes quiet sometimes venting

Mother of mine I love you so much
Without you what can I say
The man that I am I would not be
I thank you for everyday day
That you've been here for me

So on this fine day I would just like to say
Hope you have the day you deserve
But there's not enough money on earth
To thank you the way that I should

A box of chocolates a Mother's Day card
Nothing seems enough to show how I feel
So I'm just going to say I love you so much
Your the best mother without any question

So Happy Mother's Day From me to you
Your son

Stu

HAPPY

Just be happy don't be sad
Always walk around with a smile on your face
Feeling so glad releasing the mad

What will you do if happy is not for you
Be glum, be sad, be angry or be mad
Wouldnt you rather be happy
Does it sound that bad

Let the anger go
Feel the happy glow
It ain't so bad getting rid of sad
Don't let the anger blow
Replace the mad embrace the glow

Wear the smile like a crown
Now you've turned the frown upside down
Just remember not to look like a clown

Happy is the key it will make you feel free
Let your nasty go
Embrace happy and steel the show

Your smile is warm it glows like the sun
When people see it you watch it catch on
From one smile to two then more than a few
Everyone's happy the sky shines so blue

All from the smile that started with you be
HAPPY

Stu

GOODNIGHT

Red sky in the morning
It's said gives the Shepard's a warning
But how can it be
The sky is red it looks so nice to me

Will we see the blue
It's still a bit dark the red shines through
I think the clouds will go
Then the sun will show
Just how bright it really can glow

When she shines she does so bright
Feel the warmth no need to fight
Enjoy, relax, sit and chill
Have a drink have another or even two

Mornings gone clouds have too
Now it's hot in the garden or up at the plot
A bead of sweat runs down your nose
Don't forget the cream before it glows

Are you pale, grey or white
Then factor fifty may help your plight
If you have some colour in your skin
Then go lower, but it's not something that you'll win

Now it's late the sun sinks down
Causing shadows that look like frowns
Don't be sad don't be grumpy
You've had a good day with drink and food a plenty

The night brings chill but the fridge still full
Then you see an answer that brings glee
Sat in the corner an old rusty burner
Out it comes first of the year
Plenty of wood ready to burn
Go get some more I think it's your turn

Once the sun has gone to bed
You can't beat the glow of red
Sometimes sparks will fly and blow
If they Land on your skin you soon will know

So what a day you've had today
Sat in the sun beers and food
Down to the shorts not quite nude
Now your done fires burnt low
Pour on the water say goodbye to the glow
Look to the sky moon so bright
I think it's time to say

Goodnight.

Stu

GREENHOUSE

A place to go where the green will grow
You plant the seeds so small
Yet when they grow they grow so tall

Every day you go
Watching closely at what you sew
Fill the can with water
Pour on gently give them a drink
It's not like filling the sink

The water soaks into the soil
Surrounding your seeds
With what they need
Giving them the spark they seek

Some take days and some take weeks
Give them time there not as fast as weeds
But come through they will
Rewarding your watering
From all the cans that you fill

Everyday you look you check
Is there green are they popping through
Have the seeds grown
Did it help using poo

Solace paradise a real happy place
A green house a glass house
Call it what you will
When I go to my plot it's where I like to chill

I sit in my seat a deck chair you know
Looking out through the door
I can see plenty more
Radish and spuds peas and green beans
Cook them or eat them raw
There's plenty more where they came from
That is for sure

Stu

TIRED

As a kid you just don't stop
You keep on going you never flop
Legs would burn heads would turn but keep on
going your young and never slowing

You and your friends on adventures big and small
but never tired always standing tall
Walk or run short or tall you never stopped even after a fall

Years go by in your teens still not slowing beard starts showing
You just keep on going

Now in your twenty's gym all the time beers a plenty
but never slowing tired never showing

30s come but you never noticed a little bit slower and grey
hairs now showing always losing more after every shower

Into your forties back not so strong knees now
aching hair receding muscles start to weaken

Fifties come that's where I am now knees both
knackered always feeling shattered backs broke
in two that's how I feel what about you

Keep on going do what you do play your guitar cut your grass off to the plot dig over the lott don't miss the gym go out on your bike you think you'd sleep well but when your in bed you always feel wired unable to sleep even though your so

TIRED

Stu

WORDS

Everyday you do your stuff
If your like me with time
There's never enough
So rush rush rush
You won't catch me on the last push

Just a few words can tell it all
Some stories big some stories small
Each and every word required in both
Read one write one make one your own

You'll never run out there's just far too many
So just write them down
Some with a smile
Some with a frown
All words are awesome
Trust me I use them so much

So just have a go in words you can trust
There are just so many each one it's own
At first it seems hard where do I start
Just don't worry you don't have to be smart

Write them all down
They can come thick and fast
Because in your memory they just may not last
Once there gone there all in your past

Think of some more there's plenty left
They spring into your mind fast like a flash
Just like a pebble making a splash

Words can be kind of that there's no doubt
But words can be cruel harsh and unkind
Once these words are spoken there's no turning back
Out of your mouth and into the world
The ears they are meant for listen with intent
The damage is done they can't be unspoken
So just beware they can leave people broken
Words

Stu

TILL

Run till you walk
Scream till you talk
Climb till you fall
Argue till you've said it all

Dance till your still
Booze till you snooze
Drink till your drunk
Win till you lose

Drive till your there
Eat till your full
Give till it's gone
Answer till your wrong

Sing till it's sung
Swim till it's swum
Laugh till you cry
Live till you die

Stu

THE NOD

Out on the bike
not peddling long
I don't know him he don't know me
The nod

It's a language all of its own
No words spoken you don't need your phone
The nod

Doesn't matter where
Or what country your in cos all blokes know
It's the nod

It don't take much
It's just enough
The littlest of movements
But sent the right way
Over to him anytime of the day
The nod

You do it without knowing
It's just in your blood
Happy or sad
rain snow or hail
Across the road you see him
He's there and just like that
he sent you
The nod

It's not hard to do
It doesn't take much
Its more than a smile
But it means so much
The nod

So next time your out
Minding your own
Just be aware your never alone
Send him one over he'll send you one back
It'll make you feel better like a pat on the back
The nod

Stu

HAPPY BIRTHDAY

Birthdays come and birthdays go
The more you have the more you know
Everyone different never the same
But you still enjoy them sun wind or rain

What does it mean on this day
As a kid you would go out and play
But I'm not a kid anymore
My numbers large
Never been this old before

Birthday wishes from social media galore
Send a thank you back to them one and all
They all mean so much especially cards through the door
Back in the day post was the only way

Presents so nice a fortune spent
But I'm long in the tooth
Don't waste money on me
I'd much rather have you sat where I can see

Some like the fuss some just don't get it
Up in the morning soon to forget it
It's only one day in your life of so many
But on this fine day many years ago
Your mother gave birth of this we all know

So enjoy your day eat drink and laugh plenty
You deserve everything your presents they've spent on
Thank them all so much your family and friends
Because without them it's just another day
It's them that make this a special and a very

HAPPY BIRTHDAY

Stu

ALLOTMENT 4

It's been several months now
We've eaten quite a lot
We're not planting so much
But we still go up to the plot

We're fully into autumn now
All the summer fruits have gone
We've still got beds with lots to eat
It's wonderful so many treats

There's apple trees with apples on
There's turnip white as snow
The beetroots small it didn't grow
I think it was too late to sew

The bushes cut back
The trees all chopped
The winter work not quite done
But we're all waiting for spring to come

So keep going up and pulling those weeds
There the nasty ones that don't come from our seeds
Soon enough the sun will come
Then our plants will grow and that's the fun

Stu

GOOD NIGHT

Down at Dave's beers paid on
Walked so far legs so strong
What a day sun so bright
days like these have gotta be right

Bbq burning with snap on top
just keep on turning stop the burgers burning
Eat drink and be merry
The food is so good just eat plenty

The people are here more than a few
Bellies full with burgers up to your neck
There's plenty more for me and for you
food and ale all in abundance
Man cave full no chairs left
I'll stand outside the sun is the best

Are you having fun
This is a question
Think hard and strong
Please don't answer wrong

It's getting late sun now dropping
Foods nearly gone some people stopping
Dave thanks a lot it's been a great day
He won't take my money won't let me pay

Time for us to go off to the cross
It's not very far just a little walk
Doesn't take long while we all talk

Here we are off to the bar
Aka's first round cheers that's sound
Pool table empty let's have a game
Doubles well play teams now chosen
Aka pots the black I stand there frozen
Splend giggles aloud first game over

What a gang we've all known each other for so long
Talking plenty all now drunk
Laughing from your belly who needs the telly
Memories made to add to the list
I hope I remember them when I'm not pissed

Last orders called do you want another
I'm so full I couldn't drink any more
One more pint I'll be laid out on the floor

Come on then it's time to go
Let's have a walk no taxi needed
Aka goes that way and the girls say goodnight
Just Jase and I left now to walk
We stop at the snicket to stand and talk

Not the first time we've been here before
So much history built over the years
Stood for an hour it's now time for bed
See you soon my friend we both then said
It's been a very

Good Night

Stu

GOLF

Some may say greatest game in the world
Some may say spoils a good walk
Fourteen clubs in a bag
On your shoulder or wheels to shove
To the first tee don't forget the glove

Par four beckons out comes the big stick
Ball on the tee big stick in hand
Give it a whack just avoid the sand
Whoosh through the air club smacks the ball
Didn't catch it right better shout fore

Landed in the rough thick green and wet
Choose the right club or your not going far
Give it extra power or you'll never make par
Caught it sweet up in the air
landed on the fairway no need to swear

On the green in three
Twelve foot left for par for me
Out with the putter just line it up
Give it a good stroke
Avoid the sharp poke

Off it goes on the right line
All looking good balls looking fine
Then it takes a bobble Kicks to the left
Three feet to go
Misses the rim by the width of a shim

About to shout get in
Then the air turns blue
All sorts of words formed on your lips
Not to be heard by any of your kids

Tap in for bogey leave it behind
Because if you don't it'll fester in your mind

Eighteen holes later score card ruined
Too many eights a couple in the lakes
Managed three pars should have got more
Off to the 19th to talk about our scores
Walked really far now ready for the bar
Time for a pint nice cold and fizzy
That's the game of golf don't get in a tizzy

Stu

AUTUMN

Get up for work but where's the sun
It's gone very dark I feel so glum
Seems like only yesterday we were
Sat having fun with a beer in the sun

Leaves on trees start loosing their green
Before too long brown and orange are all to be seen
I have to say it's a beautiful landscape scene
Was the summer just a dream

Indian summer or so they say
Just enjoy the winter sun when there is no rain
I was lucky this year I had a holiday in Spain
That is now so far away
It seems like I hear the alarm clock every day

It's getting colder and I'm getting older
Throw over a blanket it's not that cold
I would put on the heating but it's very over sold
Enjoy the changing season even in the cold

Don't stay glum you can still have fun without the sun
Put on a coat a nice thick jumper socks to the knees
Shoes with treads like a dumpster
Go for a walk take the dog enjoy this season wait for the fog
Autumn

Stu

MY MAM

Born on hallowe'en some say a witch
but I say a queen

She's my mam what can I say
Not very tall really quite small
But don't be fooled by size
Pat Hayward born a Burton
She's no fool that's for certain
My mam

Back in the day small, blond, fiery as hell
A proper blond bombshell
Down came the big Scott from over the wall
He thinks he stands a chance She's only very small
My mam

Try he did over again until she gave in under the strain
Love soon flourished it didn't take long
Ring on the finger married soon after
Kids on the way what can you say
My mam

She's my mam love her I do
same as my brother and my father too
Eighty years young likes to have a drink
Won't stop smoking even when she's choking
My mam

There she is drink in hand
Loves to listen to a really good band
Likes a sparkly jumper hanging off her shoulder
Proud sometimes loud
Shell never hide under a shroud

My mam

So here we are from near and afar
She's my mam but Pat to you
We're all here to wish her the best
So raise your glass let's have a few
Happy birthday to my mam
From me and from you
My mam

Cheers

Stu

I DIDN'T KNOW

Hello you say as he walked you bye
Ignorant sod under your breath you say
Sod him you think as he walks away
He must be in a mood again today

She smiles so bright but no hello
Did you notice the sadness below
That smile disappeared before you passed
Is she alright or has she relapsed

Make that call use that phone
You know she's hiding something
You can hear it in her tone
But she won't say she feels alone

Everyday the pain people feel
Hidden by their mask they try to conceal
But this does not make it not real
In their head they hear their scream
It's loud and vivid just like a dream

How could you know impossible you say
But if you were bothered and less quick to chelp
You may just have noticed then you could offer them help
Of course they won't take it even if you meant it

So don't keep doing what you do
Have a second thought their people like you
Don't make a show or be cold like snow
The worst thing you can say to them is sorry
I Didn't Know

Stu

NEVER GIVE UP

Never give up you just never know
Always keep trying forget the word no
Because when you try your chances they grow
At first it seems grim god how could you win
But then in an instant they falter they flutter
Now is your chance try harder you mutter
The line is in site your opponent now stutters
You try now your hardest you've never tried more
Because your a winner it's written in your core
Your opponent now beaten it's written on their face
You've done it your a winner never thought it could be
Just look in a mirror your face full of glee
Never give up I hope you now see
That is the reason a winner you'll be

Stu

DECEMBER

December the first it's that month again
You don't really know why it's a pain
Trees in the loft it stays there all year
Go get it down say the kids in my ear

You hold off again another day gone
They just don't give up they go on and on
It's too early I say but there not having that
Just put it up dad we're going to be the last

This is because you puppets out there
Can't hold your water I find it unfair
Up goes your tree trimmings galore
Some in November don't you know the score

Then there's the show offs that really take the mik
Tree in the window and trimmings not enough
Out come the lights to shine on the house
Blow up reindeer and a sleigh on the roof
Am I too old or just too long in the tooth

I play the grinch well some think it's the truth
But inside I smile from the tips of my toes
Up through my bones to my hair that no longer grows
Believe me or not that's up to you

But let me just say that love it I do
From my kids being born seeing Santa it's true
It's this time of year I get to see you
Out in a group it only happens once

STUART ALEXANDER HAYWARD

Once every year on New Year's Day
My father my brother neighbours and friends
End up in the boozer playing snooker in twos
Then pound a man killers so easy to lose

So try to remember what the seasons about
It's not about their house looking better than yours
It's not about spending money that you ain't got
It's about meeting people you haven't seen since
Last Christmas time a year ago I hear you wince

Stu

DO IT

Just do it because you can
You don't have to do anything
But if you do they will thank you
You know it will make you feel better
It won't take you long go in the car
You know they will be in they never go far
It will make their day just look at their faces
You don't have to take pressies just you will do
You know you should go more but your always busy
It's not your fault you work all the time it's what you do
So when you get the chance just make the effort
You don't have to stay long just half an hour
That will be enough no need to be longer
Off now you go feeling much better
Your back home in five minutes
With a smile on your face

Stu

MANCHESTER

Concrete jungle so they say
Building building every day
Here for the markets what can I say
Drink some beers drink mulled wine
Time for cocktails we will be fine
Two for one you can't go wrong
Thirteen pound fifty your singing a song
Christmas music you can't escape
But why would you want to they play it very late
Lager bitter mulled wine and cider
I'll have a cocktail I'm stood right beside her
So drink we will and eat some more
It doesn't get better I'm pretty sure
We can't have a dance no room on the floor
Time to go back the hotel room beckons
A mucky kebab on the way we will have
She has garlic but chilli for me
The chillis too hot I didn't want that
Just get it down it will do you some good
We make the journey only once each year
Birmingham Newcastle Liverpool we've been
But we always return to our favourite you see
Here we are visiting Manchester city again
We think your the best and we've had a blast
We will be back soon this won't be our last
Thank you Manchester

Stu

FAR AWAY

Another one gone so fast it past
Was it a day it never seems to last
In the morning we woke
A little bit rough from beers and shorts filled with coke

Has he been cried through the house
My children tall I remember when they were small
Down the stairs they would hurry
Smiles so wide and exited all in a flurry

Presents galore pilled high to the sky
One pile for our daughter the other our son
The joy on their face can not be replaced
A tear in our eye from the joy we behold
Santa has been is what they are told

In a flash it's all over already yesterday
They look at their presents wondering what to play
So many toys the choice is so hard
Look at that box it's a tank or a car

In it they jump imagination running wild
Do they need all those toys
The box it will do now empty and void
Draw on some wheels now a car to be enjoyed

The years go by enjoy every one
The children get older where's it all gone
The laughter the screaming the paper would fly
Now there young adults so many have passed by

STUART ALEXANDER HAYWARD

So Boxing Day is here more food and more beer
Some go out to the pubs tradition we're told
I'm still recovering from yesterdays feast am I old
I'll watch the kids play on the sofa I lay
That's been Christmas the next one is so
Far Away

Stu

JAN 1

January the first a day to behold
A gathering of men from young through to old
Who will turn up as this story unfolds
Lee fisher at the bar thought I'd give him a mention
The old ones are first they never let you down
Paid the money for the table
Stood waiting why the frown

Youngest and oldest already here
Trying to play snooker there shit have no fear
The hustler and i arrive there soon after
They can't pot a ball there's money to be made
Let's play pound a man
Robs happy his days just been made

Then the trio arrive three fine looking men
Together they travel Paul Jase and Splend
Conversation flowing about memories galore
Smiles on faces and laughing out loud
Days like these are rare with such a quality crowd

Time passes by the trio go first
Then the old guard follow all gone in a burst
There's only four left
But then better late than never
A wife two kids a mother in law too
All arrive together and the boyfriend came through
The cost of my beers just gone through the roof

Pockets is done time to move on
Bottom railway that's where we're off
Pockets was dead but down here is buzzing
Full to the brim bloke on stage singing

Fancy a dance don't mind if I do
Look at him go it's me disco Stu

Beers and shots flowing in numbers too many
Sours galore apple and cherry flavours a plenty
Surrounded by family it doesn't get much better
My daughter and niece not often together
Look at those two there stunning did I mention

The hours go by I don't want it to end
We're going to move on
Me my daughter and her boyfriend
We'll see you all later a quickie in the pack
What's happened to my brother
He's tired and gone
Bernie take him home he's definitely done

So the moral of this story I'm sure you'll agree
Is let's have a party for all including you and me
If it's only once a year but everyone is there
It's better than many when people are scarce
Happy new year

Stu

DON'T

Don't wake up dead
Don't stand still while you run
Don't scream when your silent
Don't sleep while your awake
Don't bleed when your not cut
Don't go forward in reverse
Don't wipe the tears when your not crying
Don't say yes when you shake your head
Don't think no when the answer was yes
Don't forecast rain when the sky is blue
Don't give up before you start
Don't say I love you when im not in your heart
Don't say I'll meet you if you don't ask where
Just DON'T

Stu

REMEMBER

Just remember where you came from
Remember this you'll need me before I need you
Remember when I asked you and you said no
Remember that tenner I lent you
I don't remember that
I'm sure the car was here
Do you remember him
I don't remember her
I can't remember saying that
I knew you would remember that
You promised can't you remember
I can't remember agreeing to that
Your rubbish you can't remember anything
I'm sure I'd remember that though
But I don't

Stu

CALM

Calm is king
Easy to say calm down
When deep inside behind the frown
Anger is raging hot and loud
But you won't let it out
For your too proud to scare the crowd

Calmness and coolness go hand in hand
Is it easy or given at birth
Can you learn it or is it more than your worth
Some don't know the meaning of the word
The noise in their head it is too loud
Beating hard like the steps from a crowd

Calm is not an action it's a state of mind
Sometimes to keep your mouth shut feels like a grind
Avoid the people that wind you up
This will keep the calm inside
The little digs are the hardest
But you know your the calmest
You'll never be at the end of your wits
If you never let them get on your tits

Calm rules all just imagine if not
If you let it go your emotions start to rot
Calm and happy is the way to be
Ignore the clowns and the wannabes
Let them have their glory trying so hard

STUART ALEXANDER HAYWARD

Fighting with the animals in the farm
I'll let them have it while I stay so
Calm

Stu

LIFE

That's life
That's what all the people say
You're riding high in April shot down in May
So the song goes and a very good song it is

So what is this life we live
If your lucky you will live to get old
If your lucky your family will be there untold
If your lucky you've got friends that are just as old
Don't take your luck for granted
Many would swap you that are less enchanted

Did you hear about him that was unlucky
That's life
Did you know she lost her job
That's life
I can't believe my bills have gone up again
That's life
Didn't win lotto again and I'm skint
That's life

Went out for a meal with my family
Now that's life
Went to see that band with my mates
Now that's life
Went out for a few beers and a curry

Now that's life
Going on holiday next week
Now that's life

So what does it all mean
Live for today tomorrow is always tomorrow
Life is a book of memories
Do it today and put that memory in your book
Once in your book it's there to stay
It's now yours to read whenever you may
That's life

Stu

SNOW

When they land on your face you feel how cold
The life of a snow flake never gets old
Every single one has a different story to be told
When they land and settle there ready to mould
Roll them into snow men or balls to be thrown

You know when it's coming your heatings on at home
You look out of your window the clouds so grey you moan
I think it's going to snow
But you hope the clouds move on and leave you well alone

Now your comfy settled nice and warm sat at home
Just another glance is it raining no it's snow
The flakes they come but only small it will not settle
Then you look again there bigger now your fretting
They look so big now even the grinch is not sweating

Beautiful to see the wife thinks there so pretty
But just you wait and see the chaos now comes quickly
Drivers in their cars slipping while they drive too fast
Busses late now chaos reigns trains never even left there gate

Every where to see the snow so white it blinds
My garden now looks like yours even in the city
It doesn't stop it just keeps getting thicker
All the kids having fun never seen as many even in the sun
Of to the hill they go sledge under arm or sat giving his mate a tow

The excitement goes the damage all collated
The sun now shows the snow now getting melted

Clouds all gone the last snow balls thrown
Your snow man looks deflated
Let's all hope that's all we get
Of the stuff that's cold very white and very very wet
Snow

Stu

HIT IT

Pitching wedge seven iron big stick driver
Off to the range need more than a fiver
I'll pick up my mate in my car I'm the driver
It won't take long on the bypass it's wider

Twenty minutes later car parked up
Out with the clubs to the range we go
Climb up the steps receptions at the top
Pay the man your money get ready to knock

Pick your booth and then log in
Use your mobile technology it's a win
Start with the wedge and get warmed up
Then with the Severn iron my favourite club

Hit the ball then check the screen
That didn't go far it would never hit the green
Are the numbers true they look short what about you
Try hit some more make sure you follow through

Time for the big stick best in the bag
Take off the cover admire what you see
A nice long shaft that fills me with glee
Tee up the ball that will work for me

Keep your head down and pull back the beast
Now let her go swing hard and true
With lots of speed and follow through
Listen to the whoosh and then the Big Bang

A joy to behold it just can't be beat
Put down the ball and swing nice and sweet
Hit it

Stu

WORRY

Hurry scurry late again full of worry
If it rains and fills the drains
Worry can't change the season
If the clouds spoil the view
Worry won't bring the sun back to you

Worry comes slowly in your head
Now your worried when you go to bed
You toss and turn and never learn
Taking worry to your bed won't help you sleep
Before you know you hear your alarm beep

They say that worry makes you age
Takes years off your life just turn the page
You won't get rid when your full of rage
The more you worry the less you'll change

Can you change what worries you
Being worried makes you feel blue
Think of something that makes you smile
Then the worry goes away for a while
When it's gone now look there's you

You can't change the weather
You can't change the news
You can't change the bigots views
You can't change the cost of food

You can't change the people that are rude
You can't change the cost of fuel
You can't change how the politicians rule

The best you can do
Is live the life that's good for you
All of this you can do
If you choose just to loose
All of the stuff that bothers you
Then you'll learn not to
Worry

Stu

BLOSSOM

Pink white red colours galore
These are just a few we find on the floor
Look at the trees now in full bloom
Stand under the tree don't view from your room

Spring now into summer we've waited so long
The trees getting greener by the day
The sun getting higher hear the kids play
God I love this time of year you'll hear me say

Even though it's only may
Feel the warm the cold wont stay
The rain may come
The lightning may strike
The thunder may boom
It won't be long until it's June

The smell of cut grass in the air
The smell of blossom everywhere
All the veggies bursting through
Growing and sprouting at such a pace
The colours so bright puts a smile on my face

So don't walk about with your senses asleep
Look all around examine the trees
We don't live anywhere exotic
So there's not much chance of seeing a possum

But just take a minute and notice the Blossom

Stu

DARK

Darkness takes over it swallows you whole
Try as you may you seem to lose control
Thoughts in your head seem so bad you've never ever told
What can you do when you feel empty and cold

One step at a time one foot then the other
You have so much think of the good
Your head so full it feels like wood
Avoid the pain and feel the pleasure
Then go forward whatever the pressure

It's all in your mind is what they say
They see the colours but you feel so grey
You dare not let them in scared of what they would find
Is today going to be another grind
Don't watch the clock it will go so slow
Get your head down then see how fast it can go

The sun's finally here up high in the sky
It's what you love just hear those birds cry
Your soul fills with joy it makes everything better
All the bad and the clouds fade away
letting the sun shine through the grey
It's not a walk in the park

But now you can say goodbye to the Dark

Stu

BORED

School holidays we couldn't wait
Playing games on the road outside your garden gate
Top of the street play in the park
We just kept playing until it was dark

Now I'm in my fifties Where's it all gone
Not enough hours in the day
Kids don't know how to play
Where's my phone I hear them drone
Snap chat Facebook tik tok too
I'm so glad I missed them what about you

Does time go faster as I get older
Or are kids more demanding especially without there gadgets
What can I do my phones on charge I might have to think but my brains not that large I'm bored

Just chill out and read a book
Come down stairs and watch TV
Watch this program with mum and me
No that's rubbish your watching some crap
Nobody's on line I'm just so bored

So what you going to do
It's all up to you
You don't want to play pc
You dont want to watch TV
Your mates are not online
I think I know how you feel

STUART ALEXANDER HAYWARD

I heard you in your room
So loud when you roared
I'm just so
Bored

Stu

AGE

Yes I'm older much older than I was
Some say it's in the mind but I don't think that's true
I think it's in my knees my back my neck my shoulders too but that's just me it might not be you

Age is a number big or small it doesn't give a dam if your short or tall
But one thing with age of this I am sure is that my mind is my own like it or leave it I say what I see I don't suffer fools and I don't care if you don't like me

So do what you do it's only a number not a label to define you
Go to the gym as much as it hurts ride on that bike and go on that hike play a round of golf the ball won't go straight but at least you got out and through that front gate

What makes it better is mates the same age they know what your going through they have the same aches
Some more than you some maybe less but taking the piss is still just the best

So the moral of this rhyme is stop saying no all of the time
When your asked next the simple answer is yes because the number you have is not who you are
when all said and done it's only a number on this current page it does not define you it's only your
Age

STUART ALEXANDER HAYWARD

Stu

LIGHTENING

Big and bright long and white
Lighting strikes in the skies
Don't be daft you better be wise
Don't get caught out under the sky

The rain will pour you won't get wet
As long as you stay inside and just don't fret
Your dogs will shake your cats will hiss and
all the time the rain pours like piss

Some shoot across the sky spreading out
wide and thin as they pass you by
While others rage and crackle with anger straight
and thick hitting the ground like a giants stick

Then you think wow that was awesome but
don't go out it's not yet done
The noise then comes when the flash has gone
because it was hotter than the sun
Boom and rumble loud and scary that's the
thunder telling you to be wary

It then subsides and goes away
What a picture it was you might say
The clouds all gone the floors all wet
Out comes the sun to help you forget

STUART ALEXANDER HAYWARD

It wasn't really all that frightening
It was only just a bit of
Lightening

Stu

MOON

If your full of gloom
Lift up your head
Take a look at the moon

She's white she's bright
She is a glorious site
Makes you feel good inside
And oh so warm on dark dark nights

See the scars see the marks
She's been up there guarding us from harm
So bow your head or tilt your cap
Just let her know you know she's there

She never fails to shine so bright
She Never fails to climb up high
She never fails to bring a smile
She's the moon take a look
She looks better up there than in a book

Stu

HOW LONG

Nobody knows how long they have
Will you reach 60 years
Will you reach 80 years
You don't know when you will go
You may be young you may be old
Live everyday like your last I've been told
For if your lucky you will grow old

You try your best to keep yourself fit
Your out on your bike your lifting weights in the gym
You've also considered starting to swim
Is this too much though dont you think
With your fat belly your not going to sink

Strava on your phone counting the miles going by
I watch on your wrist counting heart beats adding more data to your list
Pedling hard sweat pouring out
Look where you are you know you've gone too far
How you wish you had the car

Sore again from the gym you only went on a whim
Buttocks sore from the bike might be softer on a trike
Don't stop now your doing so well
Just keep putting yourself through hell
The miles you've done you could go to the moon
Even though your Sixty soon

So if I keep on riding my bike
Pumping the weights and fishing for pike
Will I live until I'm 90 is that old can I still karaoke
Just keep doing what you do

Eat the food and have a poo
Drink the wine just make sure you make the toilet in time

Live your life the best for you
How long you have is not your choice
Doesn't matter how loud your voice
Your time will come be certain of that
You don't have nine lives like a cat
Enjoy this one it's as simple as that

Stu

WEALTH

When you look at what you have
Sometimes its easy to feel sad
His car is better than mine
His house has more rooms
His garden is much bigger

But is he happy with his lot
He argues with his wife a lot
His kids are little shits
His job is hard and lonely
He has a lot of debt

Would you want the grief
Do you like to argue
Would you change your kids
Would you like His job
Do you want those bills

Look at what you have
A wife that loves you loads
No arguments to behold
A job you like is worth a lot
And kids that are the best end of

So when you look at what they have
Don't measure wealth by the size of your wallet
Look a little closer in your home
What you have is worth more than gold

So now you know what you hold
Your wealth is worth more than you were ever sold

Stu

SEA

From the sun bed nice and warm
Pick up your snorkel it's calm no storm
The sea so blue turquoise and clean
All these colours we do see
While we're snorkelling in the sea

Wear your flip flops the sands so hot
It will burn your feet if you do not
It's not that far we will be ok
We start to walk the sand is hot
Oh my lord we better move faster
So we break out into a trot

Both feet burning in the sand
Now we're running hand in hand
Heres the sea so blue and cold
In we go our feet so warm every toe

Relief comes fast a sigh sneaks out
The sea is cold but in you go
Where are the kids to see you dip your big toe
Ooohs and aaahhhs the deeper you go
Where's the wife she's already gone
The time you take she's seen the fish everyone

Past your bits deeper you get
Just dive in it's easy when your wet
Snorkel on up past your waste
In you go now at a pace

The sea so blue you can sea so far
Look at the fish that ones shaped just like a star

Schools of fish everywhere you look
Little ones swimming around your foot
Then the big ones go darting bye
You can't get near there just too shy
Beautiful vast and there was lots to see
While we were swimming in the
Sea

Stu

WET

Look at the sky it's not very clear
Is it going to rain again at this time of year
Oh yes here it comes the drops of rain so clear
The ground gets wet the puddles so deep
Unless we have floods there's nothing here to fear

The reservoirs so dry has the summer been that warm
I have a friend at work got stung by bees in a swarm
So let the rain pour don't get down we need even more
Everything is wet but look at the plants how green they get
My grass no longer brown when I look at it now I no longer frown

Looking through the window the trees now bending in the breeze
Let's all be thankful it is still summer we're not going to freeze
So on my four days off I won't moan and groan
It's only British weather you know how it goes
Just be bloody thankful the allotment grows and grows

So the moral of this story is let the rain pour
We need all the water just avoid the puddles on the floor
If your going out put on your coat and hat
For then you will find and this I will bet
That you will stay dry and not get
WET

Stu

GOBBY

He's so gobby that guy that we all know
He's always got the answer but he never steels the show

Gobby gobby sit yourself down
Gobby gobby please take off the crown

When he's here he always shouts his gob
But nobody listens because his talking
makes you want to sob

He thinks he's the man
He always knows best
But let me tell you this
He's nothing but a pest

When he turns his back
The people they all snear
And don't let him catch you
When he's had a load of beer

Stu

ANOTHER DAY

Cards and presents that's how it starts
Open them all some are large and some are small
They all mean a lot put the money from
the cards in your holiday pot

Some cards with money scratch cards in a few doesn't
matter to me you all know i love a verse or two
Every card I read every word that is wrote thank you
very much they bring a lump to my throat

People make a fuss and it's beautiful to behold but
it's just another day if the truth be told
Another one added on my total years if I think
too hard I think it could bring tears

I'm always overwhelmed at the care that is shown
it's days like these that show your not alone
To have family and friends who care for you so much it
really makes you realise just how much your loved

So thank you to you all for the birthday wishes that
you have sent I can't really say how much that they
all meant I don't have the words that's not easy for
me to say but let me tell you this it wasn't just
Another Day

Stu

PUPPY

We just got a puppy
He's daft as a brush
Bounces here and there always in a rush
Loves to bite his toys and fight with the boys

Likes to lick the cat poo and eats it from the tray
He thinks it's Cadburys chocolate
Disgusting you might say

Fluffy long and gangly pounces on every call
Thin long an bony hope he doesn't fall
Sits now to order but always wants a treat
Just look into his eyes he really is so sweet

Stu

MORE WORDS

I can't help the words I get in my head
I have to write them down you know because I said

But what if I didn't write them down
Would you be bothered would you show me your frown

It doesn't make a difference if I write or if I don't
But I can't help it of this I know

Read them ignore them it's no problem to me
I'm still going to write them just you see

If you don't like them then read no more
But if you do there are loads more thats for sure

So ill thank you if you read them
But I won't if you dont

Thank you

Stu

SNOOZE

As I lay on my sofa today
The sky is blue I don't really know what to do
Should I play on my game
Should I search for stardom and fame
I think I need some tablets for the pain

The sun is bright it's such a beautiful sight
It's beams breaking through clouds like lasers in the night
Thier shadows cast on the ground below
You can't believe they don't just drop like snow

I need to move to get in a groove
But just can't seem to shake the snooze
So stay I will flat on my back
Sofa soft and blanket covered
I'm getting hungry what's in the cupboard

I need to move and make some food
What to have I just don't know
Toast or a sandwich a pot noodle to go
A fish finger sandwich I think
Because thats the winner as you all know

Stu

TODAY

Time is precious it passes so fast
Enjoy each day they just don't last
Today is now tomorrow your future
Yesterday is your past it went so fast

Enjoy the company that you keep
For if you don't these are not
the people you should see
Is it them or is it me

Time on your own is when your alone
But time on your own is not the same
As being the only one and not the lonely one
Make the most of the time you have

Too late now to do that today
I'll do that tomorrow when I have more time
Shall we go next week instead
I can't be bothered today I need a lay in bed

I'll do it now and then it's done
When it's complete you feel like you've won
Tomorrow never comes it's always today
Next week may as well be a year away

So the moral of this story is
Today is the day before it goes away
Yesterdays gone it never comes back
And tomorrow is the future we'll never see that

So before your time passes away
Always make sure you live for
Today

Stu

MISTY

She came from a house dirty inside
Her mum and dad being bread all the time
We rescued her from hell and squalor
Brought her home to meet our Mack
He wasn't happy and he turned his back

They slept in the hall his back against the wall
She lay against his belly his legs long enough for wellies
Try as he might she really was a delight
He tried his best to think she was a pest
But Misty knew she wouldn't rest
Until mates they were the very best

Our Mack he left us what a dog
Misty didn't know where he had gone
She looked and looked but he wasn't there
Now she's gone back to her friend
Up in heaven looking down below
Barking like mad just as they did in the snow

Our little dog Misty in our lives so long
Fourteen years where's that gone
Our hearts left broken for god knows how long
You were our baby for so long
The tears we shed sting our cheeks
I'm sure there will be more over the coming weeks

She loved her food that's a fact
We gave her too much but so what
She was fourteen with a cuddly rop
I would lay her in my arm and rub her belly warm

She sat and barked she always wanted more

In the kitchen lamb in the oven
She wouldn't move she knew what was coming
Of to the plot she loved so much
Chomping on apples but her favourite to come
A juicy big carrot yum yum yum

Bye bye Misty we loved you so much
In our hearts you will stay missed so much
Our little fluffy baby we stroked so much
Waiting at the door we couldn't go without a touch
Wagging tail when we walked through the door
We will never get that anymore
Love you Misty
From all your family

Stu

BEAUTY

Beauty is in the eye of the beholder I think you will all agree
But what is it that makes that beauty for me or
that beauty for you do you know or can you see I'm
just an ordinary man but that's just me

What is she doing with him he's defo punching
He'd better get to the gym and start doing
some crunching instead of being
Sat at home eating crisps drinking wine and
doing plenty of pizza munching

Beauty comes in many forms throughout the human race
It's not just all about who has the pretty face the model
looks we see so much on tv and the front of books

Physical beauty there is no doubt it's programmed in hear the
whistles and hear the shouts but is that what it's all about
The stunning model who looks the part is not much
good sat at home with a cold black heart

So beauty that is only skin deep just be careful they may
not be the one to keep for beauty that is deep and true
comes from inside people that are just like you

Stu

SORRY

So sorry to hear about you
I hope you'll be ok
I only heard about you just the other day
When did you find out
Have you caught it early
Are you having treatment
Have you got to have some chemo

Yes I have got cancer
It's in my prostate gland
Please don't say your sorry
But don't stick your head in the sand

I don't require your sympathy
But your concern is so heart felt
Talk to me about it
I'll tell you if you ask

I'm not going to hide it
That's not how I am
You may need to know about it
From the needles to the scan

I have cancer in my prostate
But it's early and not spread
I really am so lucky
Of this I have no doubt
So please don't say your sorry
Don't shed your tears for me
I really am quite healthy
So just raise your glass for me
One thing is for certain
I just can't hold my pee

Stu

MO

The time has come to grow a Mo
But how long does it need to grow
Does it grow and grow into the longest Mo
Or do we trim so we don't look grim

Movember for the bros
Raising cash and lots of dough
Stop the suicides help with the strain
So much pain all in the brain

How much do you give
It doesn't make a difference even just a quid
It's all about the message getting it through

We need to make sure that he gets the help
Don't just stand there full of chelp
Grow a Mo your brothers need your help

Thank you for your money
I hope my Mo looks really funny
Let's have a laugh along the way
There's too much sadness in this world today

Stu

FEAR

There's nothing to fear but fear itself
But that's easier said than done
Fear comes from many things
Some you know there in your mind
Other fear comes that's not so kind

What is fear and how does it work
It's that feeling of dread that you just can't shed
Some may tremble shake or sweat
You can't control your feelings of dread
The blood runs fast it pumps in your head

Some feelings of fear maybe dreams there so clear
You wake up wide eyed
Grabbing your partner by your side
These are nightmares that you've had
Sometimes screaming like your mad

But what about the fear that freezes you stiff
It maybe your just standing looking over the cliff
When the fear triggers it's hard not to shake
But is the decision really yours to make
When all that you feel is your life is at stake

So do you grab the spider or pick up the snake
Because fear is real when you start to shake
So how do you conquer this feeling of dread
Keep away from the spiders that lurk in the shed

Somethings that scare you are worse in your head
So just look a bit deeper into what causes that dread

Stu

PROSTATE

I need to write a poem about my prostate gland
How will I do it I don't know where I stand
But the prostate is the star of the show
Have I to tell you why
I've been of to the hospital
And they have had a little spy

My prostate is not healthy
It gives me lots of pain
Is it really poorly or am I just insane
I get my test results tomorrow
Will I be full of glee
Or teary eyed with sorrow
We will have to see

Ive had lots of needles they stuck them in both arms
They've taken lots of blood the tests they worked a charm
The numbers they came back with were not very pleasing
When they fukin told me I almost started wheezing

So what is going to happen I really just don't know
But one thing is for certain it may just have to go
If I'm lucky with fingers crossed it's nothing really nasty
If the doctor says to me I'm sorry but it's past it
Then my prostate I say to you
Good bye your going in the waste basket

So it's not all bad it's glass half full fantastic
My prostate is poorly they have no doubt
It has the dreaded cancer
I just want to scream and shout
But it's the best that it could be

I could still be a dancer

No treatment needed
No removal
That comes with the doctor's approval
So raise a glass hip hip hooray
I am so thank full for today
Listen now to what I say
Please go and have a PSA

Stu

CANCER

It's that word nobody wants to hear
Just one word causes so much fear

Where has he got it has she got long left
That's all we hear all through the year

He's just had his treatment it all went well
She's just having chemo she's been through hell

They took out his tumour but it doesn't look good
She had them both removed they just said that she should

The damage that it causes has no bounds
It can come in big or small doses depending on your luck

Once it gets a grip your gonna need some luck
So anything abnormal your doctor needs a look

Treatments getting better of this there is no doubt
But if you choose to ignore it you could end up losing out

So what is it I'm saying your all too busy playing
You think that you'll be fine the doctors busy all the time

I'll make it just quite simple any lump or pain you gain
The doctor needs to see you if not you must be insane

It's not going to go away it's going to get much worse
If you don't sort it out your funeral is where I'll read this verse

Stu

AFTERMATH

Your results are in it's not looking good
The big C has landed your thinking oh fugg
But glass half full it's not that bad
No chemo or radio needed so don't be sad

Your heads all mixed up you can't think straight
Just don't panic you'll lose more weight
Worry not it's the best it could be
It's not getting me fugg the big C

Up and down your emotions are raw
Sometimes I smile I think I'm all good
But sometimes I don't smile
I feel like I could cry well maybe I should

A few weeks gone by the news is still new
It will take another week maybe even a few
It will get easier when your head gets in gear
It makes it much easier now your not living in fear

You may get pissed off and snap at your mates you
may even get angry and chelp at the wife some might
say your no different but what do they know
It's not fugging easy let me tell you so

The damage it's done
The pain it's caused

Don't let it win don't walk down its path
It's all up to you to stop the
Aftermath

Stu

ACKNOWLEDGEMENT

This book has been a long time in coming. I have been told by many people that I should put my poems into a book. I have to thank Amazon to start with, because without their self publishing service this would not be something that an ordinary working bloke like me could really do.

It would be hard to acknowledge all the people by name so I am not going to try. That said I do thank all of you that have supported me along the way with my poems. If you only read one, but commented on that one then you are still part of my journey that led me here with this book.

This book is really special to me, and it has a lot of my heart and soul in it. It covers good times and hard times, and for you the family and friends that have just given that thumbs up, or that well done, I like that, then I thank you so much, I can not put into words what that support has meant to me. My Brother Andy, Jase, Paul, Dave and Glen you jokingly call me "the Barnsley Bard" thank you, you have no idea how much that actually means to me. My always fans, Terry and my Mum and Dad, Love Stu.

ABOUT THE AUTHOR

Stuart Alexander Hayward

Stuart Alexander Hayward comes from a small village in Yorkshire. He was a clever child but never really tried at school. He came in to his own when he became an apprentice Electrician after leaving school. At collage during his apprenticeship he excelled getting top marks through most of his college years, ending up with a HNC in Electrical and Electronic Engineering. He loves technology and has been a qualified Electrician for almost forty years.

Stuart met his wife Terry whilst working at the same factory. They were soon engaged, married and have two children. Both Stuart and his wife are very family orientated and love animals.

Stuart has many hobbies which include writing, going to the gym, riding his bike, playing golf, guitar, and playing all kinds of arcade games across many platforms including retro.

BOOKS BY THIS AUTHOR

My Prostate Story, Does It Stay Or Does It Go.

My Prostate Story, is Stuart Alexander Haywards first published book. This is his story that is heart on sleeve stuff. He details it all from the first doctors appointment to his final diagnosis of Prostate Cancer.

It is funny, sad, heart worming and will have you not knowing whether to laugh or cry along the way.

It is a must read for anyone that has been on the same journey or just starting out on their cancer journey.

Printed in Great Britain
by Amazon